HOW MANY FROGS?

A first maths book

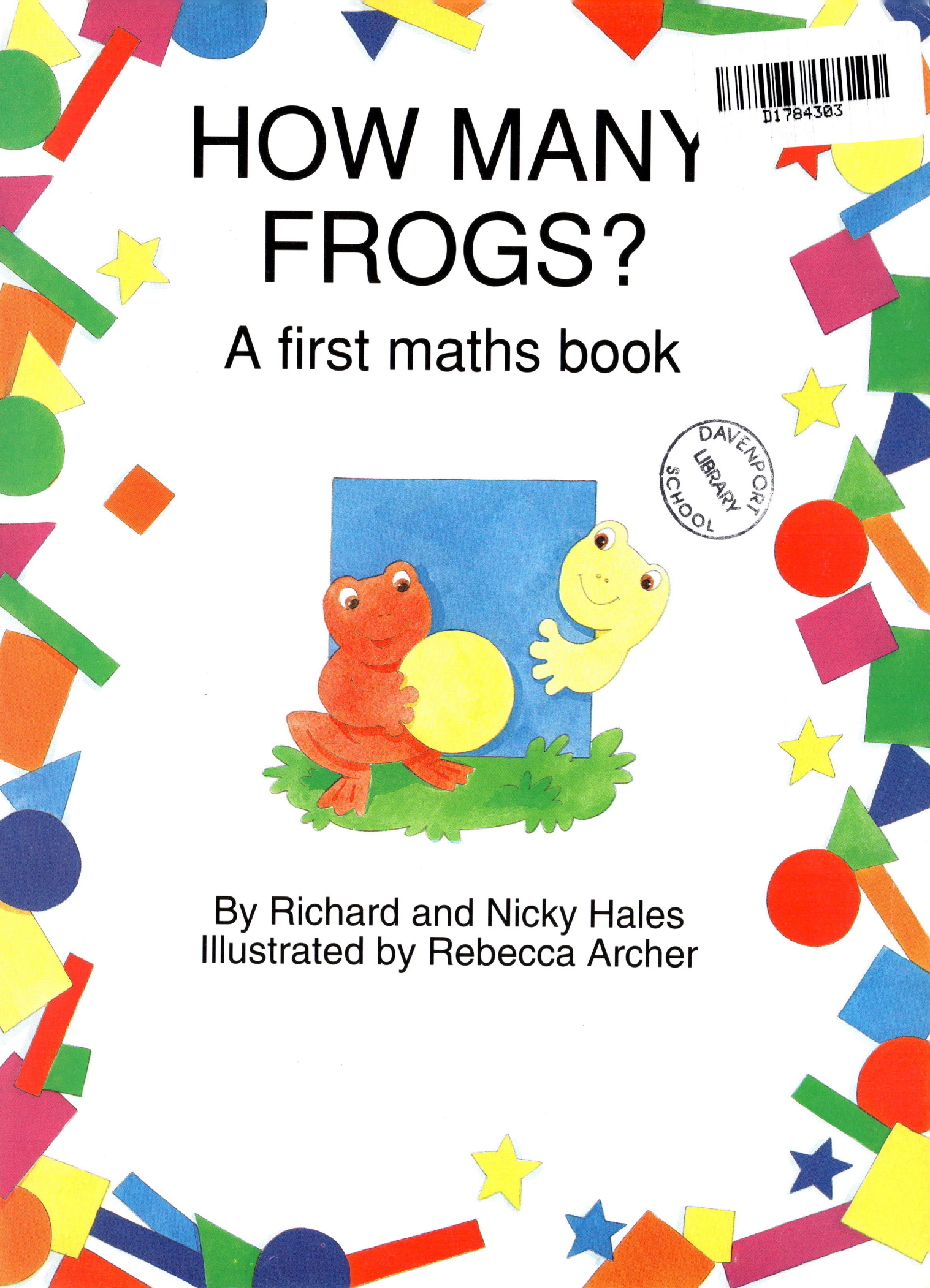

By Richard and Nicky Hales
Illustrated by Rebecca Archer

HOW MANY FROGS?

Have fun with these mathematical frogs.

Look at shapes.
    Spot the difference.
        Work out what comes next.
            Learn how to add.
                Tell the time.
Play games and solve puzzles.

Try to answer the questions in the book but do not write in the book. Put your answers on a piece of paper.

There are answers to the questions at the bottom of each page, but you will have to turn the book upside-down to read them. Try not to look before you have had a try.

If your answer is wrong, try again. If it is still wrong, you may still be right. Sometimes there is more than one answer.

CONTENTS

Shape 5

What's the difference? 15

Adding 25

What's next? 35

What's the time? 45

Puzzles and games 55

A Cherrytree Book

Designed and produced by A S Publishing

First published in 1996
by Cherrytree Press Ltd
a subsidiary of Chivers Press Ltd
Windsor Bridge Road
Bath BA2 3AX

British Library Cataloguing in Publication Data

Hales, Richard, 1953-
How Many Frogs?
1. Mathematics – Juvenile literature
I. Title II. Hales, Nicky
510

ISBN 0 7451 5299 6

Printed in Malaysia

SHAPE

Do you know these shapes?

square

triangle

oblong

circle

Folding shapes

You need three square pieces of paper.

Can you fold one square to make two oblongs?

How many folds do you need to make 2 oblongs?

You need 1 fold to make 2 oblongs.

6

Can you fold another square to make two triangles?

Can you fold another square to make four squares?

You need 1 fold to make 2 triangles.
You need 2 folds to make 4 squares.

Squares

You need some short straws.

Make a square with four straws.

Make a bigger square with more straws.

Are all the squares the same size?

How many straws did you use?
How many squares have you made?

You need 12 straws to make 5 squares.
There are 4 small squares and 1 large square.

1	2
3	4

5

How many straws do you need to make this square?

How many squares have you made now?

How many large ones?

How many small ones?

Triangles

Use three straws to make a triangle.

Add more straws to make a bigger triangle.

How many straws did you use?
How many triangles have you made?
Are they all the same size?

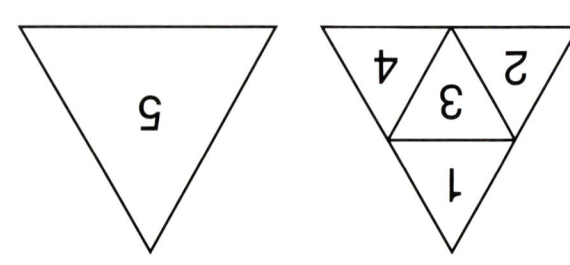

You need 9 straws to make 5 triangles: 4 small triangles 1 large triangle.

10

Add more straws to make this triangle.

How many straws did you use?
How many triangles have you made?
How many large ones?
How many small ones?

You need 18 straws to
make 13 triangles:
9 small triangles
1 large triangle
3 medium triangles.

Oblongs

You need some oblong domino shapes.
You can use real dominoes or make your own.
They need to be twice as long as they are wide.

How many different patterns can you make
with four dominoes?

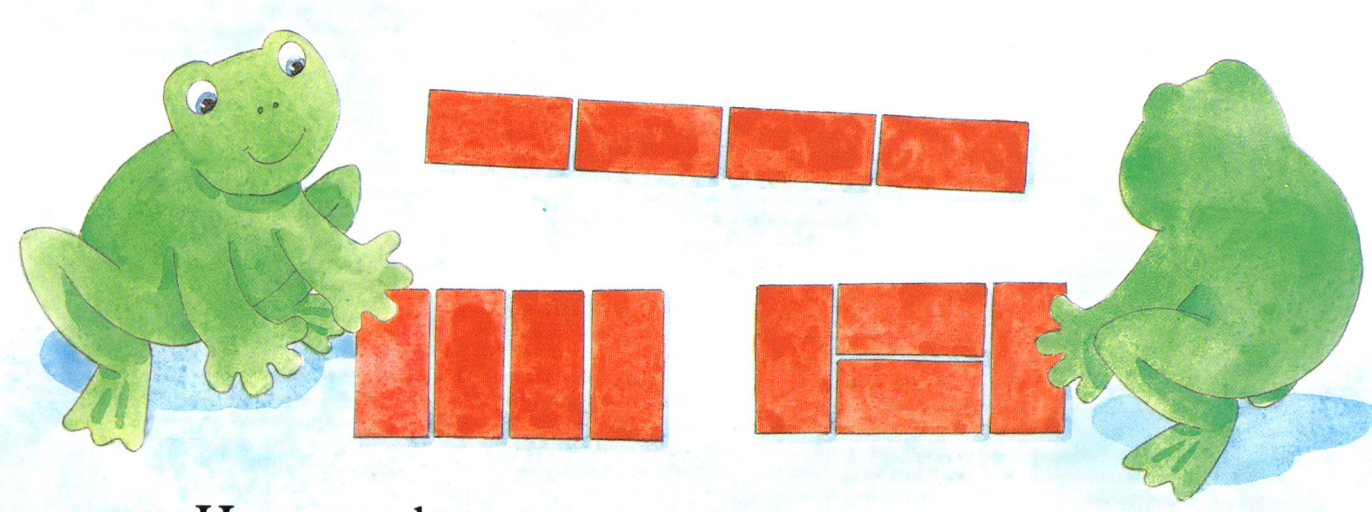

Here are three patterns.
How many more can you make?

Here are two 4-domino patterns.

How many patterns can you make with six
dominoes?
Here is one pattern.

Here are six 6-domino patterns.

Boxes and tins

Collect some containers from your kitchen.

Sort out the shapes with square faces.
Sort out the shapes with oblong faces.
Sort out the shapes with round faces.

Choose one of the containers.
Draw round one of its faces on a piece of paper.
Draw it again and again to make a pattern.
Make sure the faces touch each other.

WHAT'S THE DIFFERENCE?

We are twins.
We both like swimming.
We are almost the same.

Can you see a difference between us?

Look at these two pictures.
Are they the same?

Can you find six differences
between them?

We found
five. Can
you find
one more?

There are six differences.

One blue frog has changed costume.

The ball has changed colour.

One rail is missing from the steps.

One red frog has changed costume.

One yellow frog is missing.

One towel has changed colour.

Odd one out

Which is the odd one out?

Why is it different?

Which of these is odd? Why?

The frog is odd in a set of objects.

The ball is odd in a set of animals.

Which of these is odd? Why?

The ice-cream is odd in a set of fruit.
The pepper-pot is odd in a set of cutlery.
The plate is odd in a set of drinking vessels.
The bucket is odd in a set of clothes.

How many?

How many frogs are there?
How many rubber rings are there?

Does every frog have a ring?

There are 4 frogs.
There are 3 rings.
No, every frog does not have a ring.

20

How many frogs are there?
How many beach-balls are there?

How many frogs haven't got a ball?

There are 5 frogs.
There are 3 balls.
There are 2 frogs without a ball.

More or less?

How many frogs are diving?
How many frogs are swimming?

How many more frogs are swimming than diving?

Two frogs are diving.
Four frogs are swimming.

Two more frogs are swimming than diving.

How many frogs are sliding?
How many frogs are floating?

How many more
are sliding
than
floating?

Five frogs are sliding.
Two frogs are floating.
Three more frogs are sliding than floating.

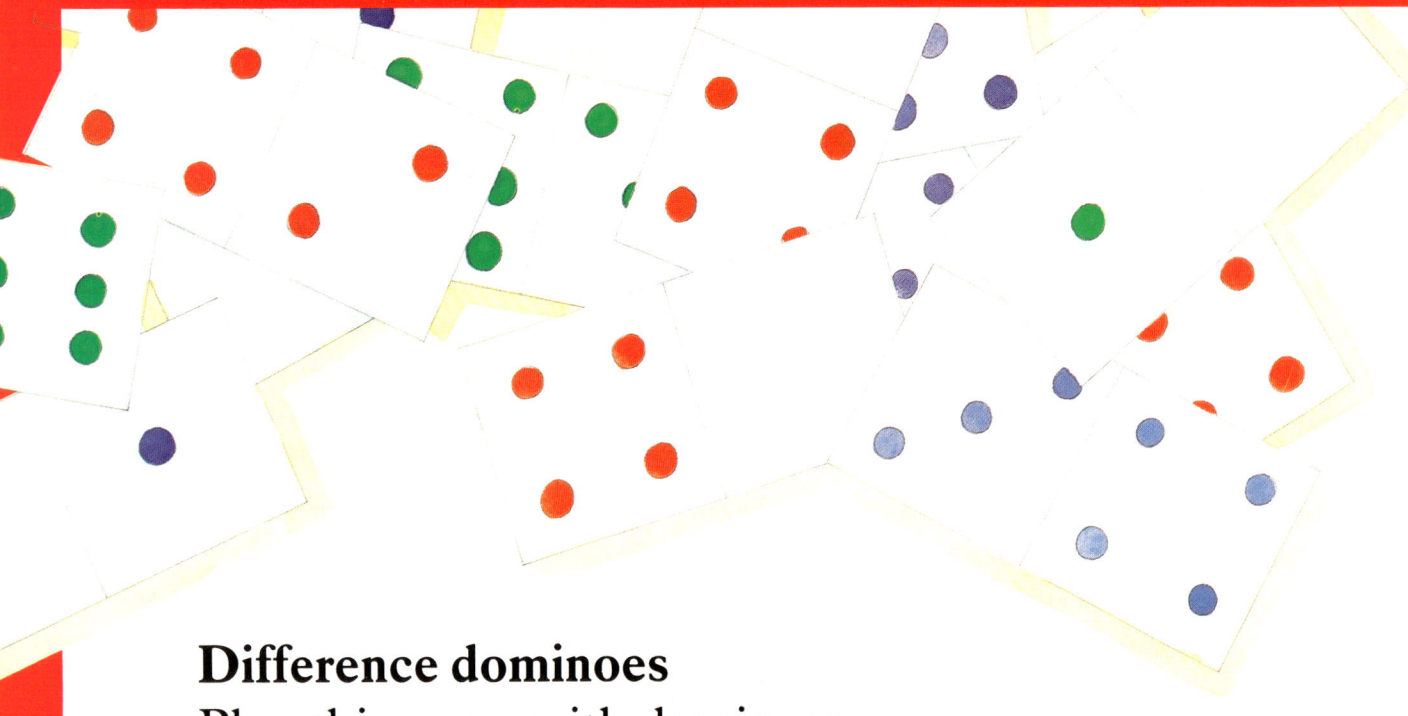

Difference dominoes

Play this game with dominoes.
Put one domino down.
Lay a domino that is one different next to it.
It can have one more or one less spot.

The winner is the first person to lay all of his dominoes.

Now try playing two-difference dominoes.

ADDING

What are these frogs doing?
How many are playing on the climbing frame?
How many are playing on the roundabout?
How many frogs are there altogether?

What are these frogs doing?
How many red frogs are there?
How many yellow frogs?
How many frogs are there altogether?
How many frogs are in tunnels?
How many frogs in a tyre?

There are 6 red frogs.
There are 5 yellow frogs.
There are 11 frogs altogether.
Two frogs are in tunnels.
One frog is in a tyre.

How many frogs are riding bikes?
How many frogs are driving cars?
Are more frogs riding bikes than driving cars?
How many more?
How many frogs are there altogether?

Five frogs are riding bikes.
Four frogs are driving cars.
There is one more frog riding a bike than driving a car.
There are 9 frogs altogether.

On the lily-pad

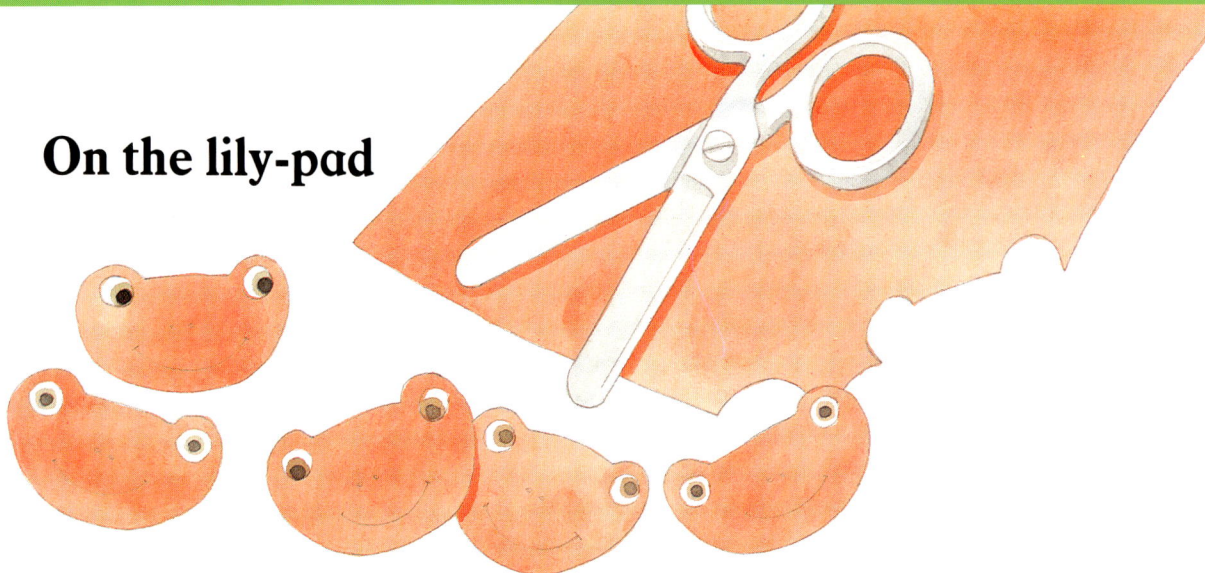

Cut out five frogs from cardboard.
Draw two water lilies.

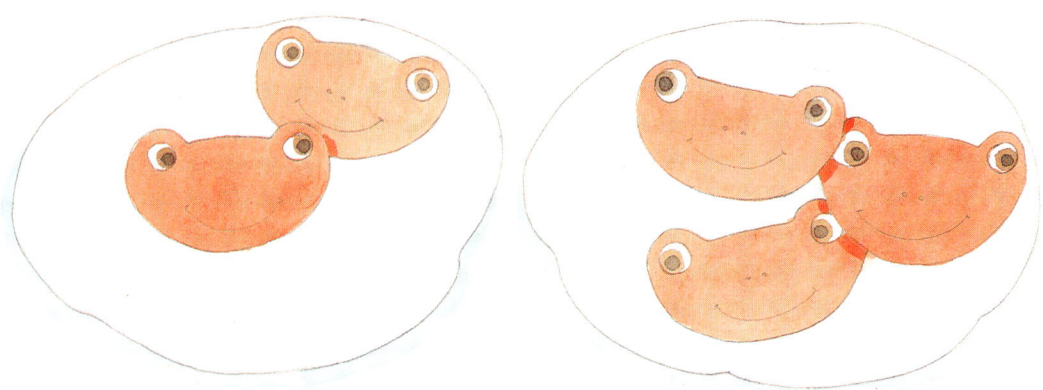

How many ways can you put the frogs on the
lilies?

Suppose there were more frogs.
Suppose there were 6 frogs.
How many ways could they go on the lilies?

If there were five frogs,
they could go like this:

- 0 and 5
- 1 and 4
- 2 and 3
- 4 and 1
- 5 and 0

If there were six frogs,
they could go like this:

- 0 and 6
- 1 and 5
- 2 and 4
- 3 and 3
- 4 and 2
- 5 and 1
- 6 and 0

Magic squares

Magic squares have numbers that add up the same in all directions.

Can you put these numbers into a square so that each row, column and diagonal adds up to 6?

Make other magic squares and find out more about them.

Use 2,2,2 and 3,3,3 and 4,4,4.

Now try 3,3,3 and 4,4,4 and 5,5,5.

Each row, column and diagonal add up to nine.

3	4	2
2	3	4
4	2	3

Each row, column and diagonal add up to twelve.

4	5	3
3	4	5
5	3	4

Elevenses

This is a game you can play on your own with a pack of cards.

Take out the picture cards. Shuffle the rest.

Deal out 8 cards face up.

Look for a pair of cards which add up to 11.

When you find a pair, deal a new card on to each.

Carry on until you have used up all the cards.

If you can use them up, it means you have won.

WHAT'S NEXT?

What's next?

red lorry   yellow lorry   red lorry

Can you say this quickly over and over again?

What do you think will happen next?

What do you think will happen next?

Draw what comes next on a piece of paper.

Monday   **Tuesday**   **Wednesday**

What day comes next?

Night follows day.

Thursday comes after Wednesday.

spring

summer

autumn

Draw what you think will be
in the last picture.

The frog is going to paint a picture of winter.
Why don't you do the same!

first second third fourth ?

short

shorter

shortest

long longer ?

The last frog came fifth.

The dog on the right is the longest.

What time is it?

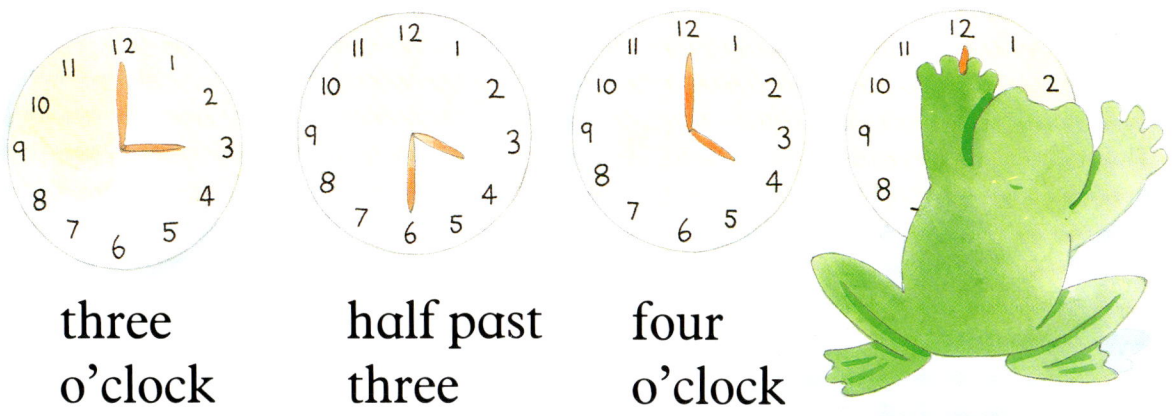

three
o'clock

half past
three

four
o'clock

What month comes next?

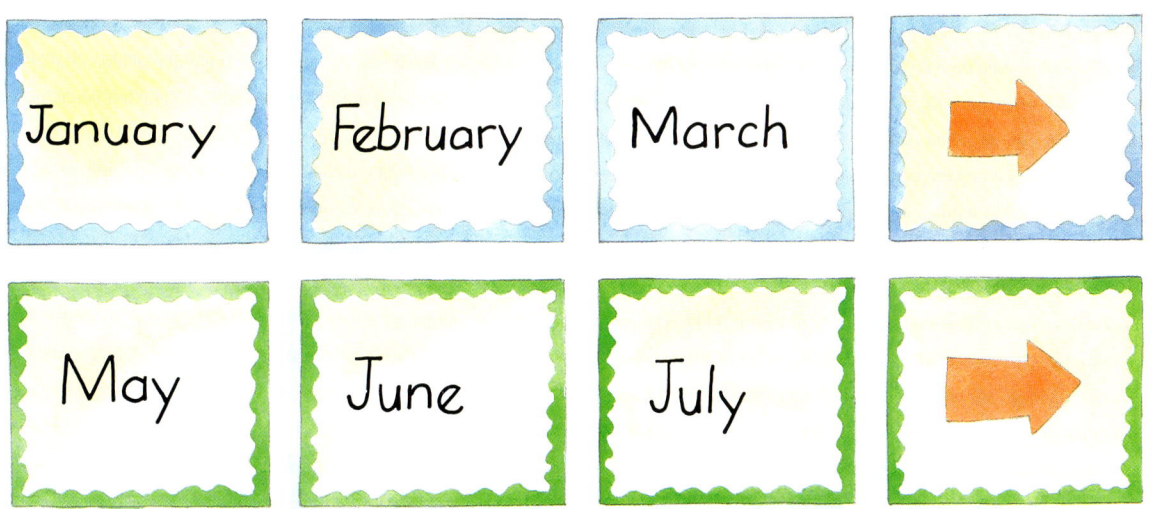

| January | February | March | → |
| May | June | July | → |

Can you go on to the end of the year?

What number comes next?

5 10 15 20 →

10 20 30 40 →

Can you go all the way to 100?

The next number in the top line is 25.

The next number in the bottom line is 50.

What number does the blue frog live at?

What number does the green frog live at?

14 7 10 13

Too hard for me!

Whatever next?

The number after 13 is 16. Just add 3.

The green frog lives at number 25.

The blue frog lives at number 24.

WHAT'S THE TIME?

What are these? What do they do?

How many days are there in a week?

There are seven days in a week.

There are 12 numbers
on a clockface.
There are 24 hours in a day.
To tell the time for the whole day
the hands go round twice.

A day is made of hours.
How many hours are in a day?

An hour is made of minutes.
How many minutes are in an hour?

A minute is made up of seconds.
How many seconds are in a minute?

How many times can you touch your toes in a minute?

There are 24 hours in a day.
There are 60 minutes in an hour.
There are 60 seconds in a minute.

School again!
It is time to wake up.
What time do you
wake up?

What time do you
start school?

The frog wakes at 8 o'clock in the morning.

He starts school at 9 o'clock.

What time do you
have lunch?

What time do you
go home?

The frog has lunch at 12 noon.

He goes home at 4 o'clock in the afternoon.

Cut out a circle of
paper.
Fold it in four and
flatten it.
Write the numbers on
the clockface.

Cut out a long hand
and a short hand.
Fix them to the face
with a paper clip.

Point the short hand at 3.
Point the long hand at 12.
What time does your
clock say?

The clock says 3 o'clock.

Can you make your
clock say 6 o'clock
or 4 o'clock or 10 o'clock?
Leave the long hand at 12.
Move only the short
hand.

What time
do these
clocks say?

Now move the long hand as well.
The long hand says how many minutes have gone.

At half-past one the hands look like this.
The long hand points to 6.
Thirty minutes have gone past the hour.

What time do these clocks say?

When the long hand points
to 3 it is quarter-past
the hour.
What time do these
clocks say?

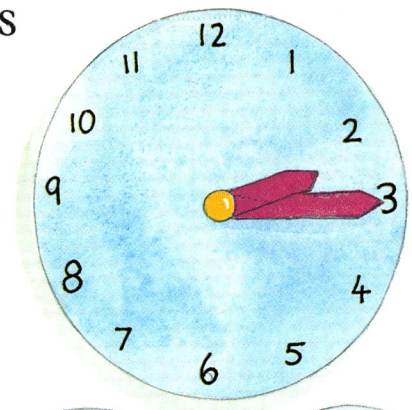

  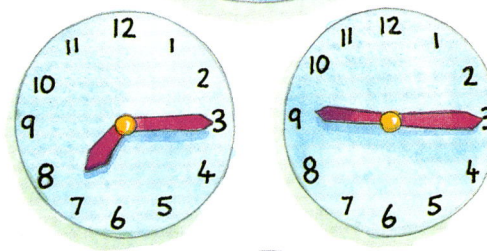

Where will the long
hand be at quarter-to?
What time do these
clocks say?

The big clock at the top says 2.15.
The ones below it say:

12.15   11.15   7.15   9.15

The other big clock says 1.45.
The ones below it say:

3.45   11.45   5.45   12.45

This is a digital clock.
It is a 24-hour clock.
At 1 o'clock in the afternoon it says 13.00.
What time does it say at 6 in the evening?

At 6 o'clock in the evening it says 18.00.

PUZZLES AND GAMES

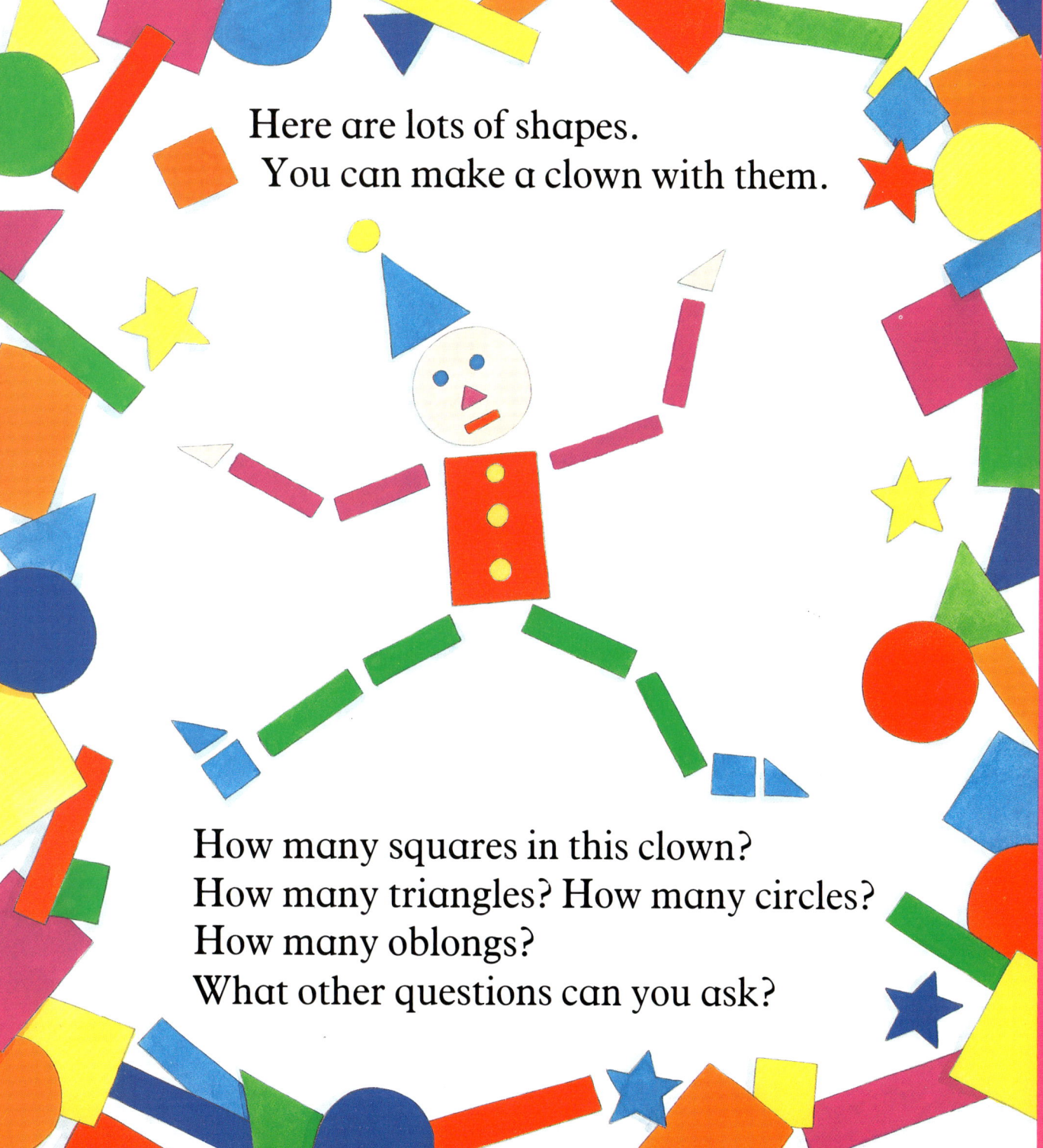

Here are lots of shapes.
You can make a clown with them.

How many squares in this clown?
How many triangles? How many circles?
How many oblongs?
What other questions can you ask?

Straw triangles and squares

You need some short straws.
Make a triangle with some of them.
How many straws did you use?

Now make another triangle, and another.

Make more triangles.

Count how many straws you use each time.

Do you notice a pattern?

Use your straws to make this shape.

Make this pattern.

Make this pattern.

How many straws?

How many straws?

Can you see a pattern in the numbers?

Straw squares
You need four straws
to make one square.
You need 3 more
straws for each
additional square.
This makes your
number pattern go
4 7 10 13

Straw triangles
Having made one
triangle from three
straws, you need two
more straws for each
additional triangle.
This makes your
number pattern go
3 5 7 9 11

The Nim game

You need 2 players and 12 counters.
Set out the counters like this in three rows.

Each player takes it in turn to pick up any
number of counters from any one row.
The winner picks up the last counter.
When you are really
good at this game,
you can change
the rules. Make
the player who
picks up the
last counter
the loser.

Crossings

How many crossing points can you make with three straight lines?

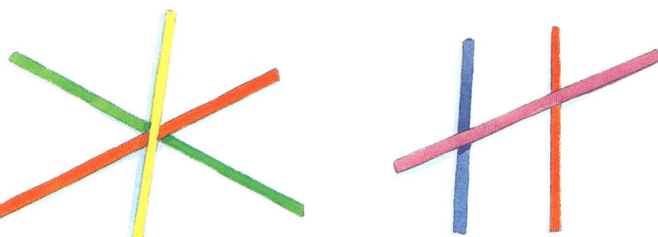

One or two or more?

How many crossing points can you make with four straight lines . . . or five . . . or more?

With three lines you can make three crossings.
With four lines you can make six crossings.

59

Darts

Make a dart board like this.
You need three counters or buttons.
These are your darts.
Drop the darts on the board to score.
Every one must land on the board.

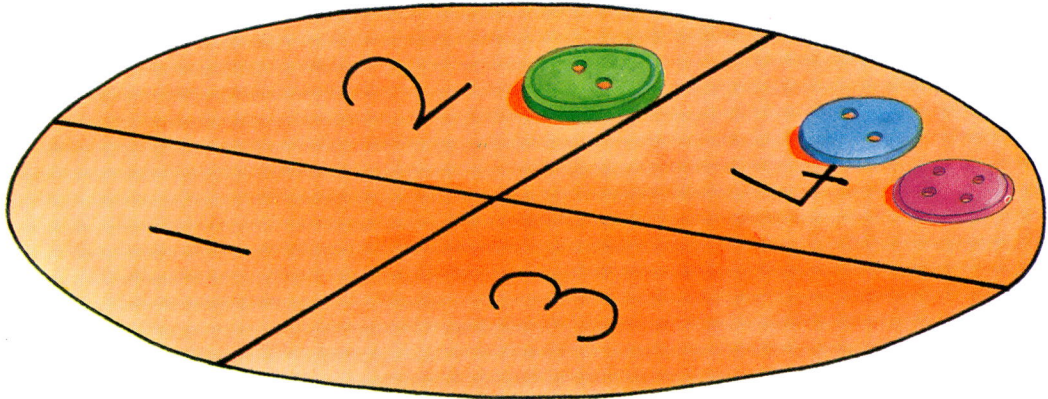

What has this player scored?
What is the lowest score you can make?
What is the highest?
Can you make every score in between?
Make your own board with different numbers.

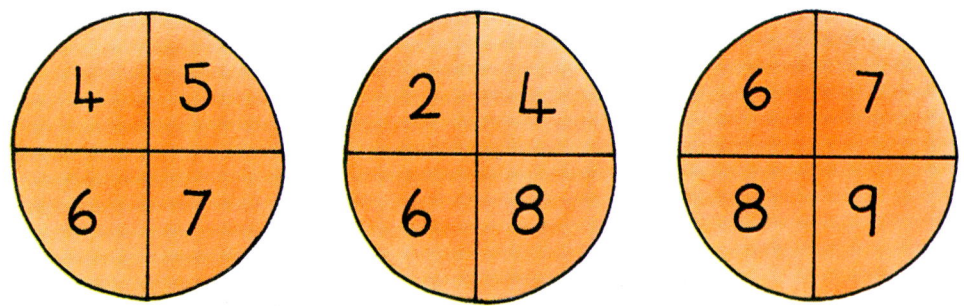

The player has scored ten.
The lowest score you can make is three.
The highest is twelve.
You can make all the numbers in between.

60

Magic marbles

The magician has two pockets and two marbles.
How many ways can he hide the two marbles?
He could hide both in his left-hand pocket.

How many other ways could he hide them?
How could he hide three marbles or more?

If the magician has two
marbles he can hide them
like this:

Left pocket   Right pocket
2   0
1   1
0   2

If the magician has three
marbles he can hide them
like this:

Left pocket   Right pocket
3   0
2   1
1   2
0   3

Leap frog

Draw this pattern on a piece of paper.
Cut out 6 frogs. Make 3 red and 3 green.

Set the frogs out like this.

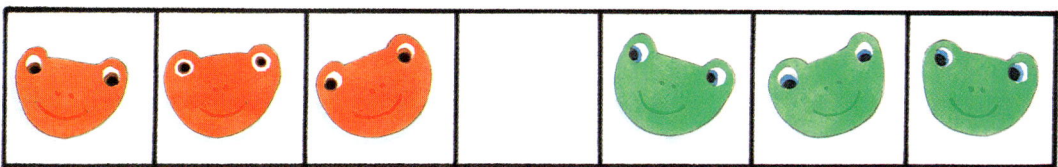

Frogs can slide to an empty square.
Frogs can jump to an empty square over frogs
of the opposite colour.

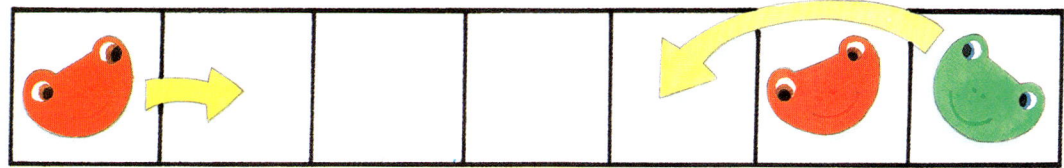

Can you make the frogs change ends?
How many moves?
How many jumps?
How many slides?

Think of a number

Try this game on your friends.

Think of a number. (Make it an easy one to begin with.)

2 → add 1 → double it → take away 2 → take away the number you first thought of

What is the answer?
Does it always work?